6/09

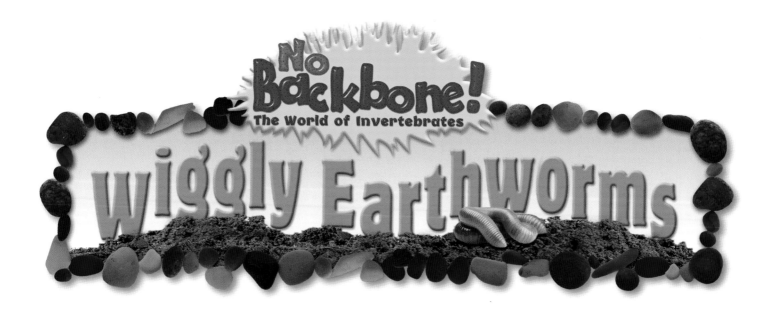

No Backbone!
The World of Invertebrates

Wiggly Earthworms

by Natalie Lunis

Consultants:

Dr. John W. Reynolds
Oligochaetology Laboratory
Kitchener, Ontario, Canada

Patricia S. Sadeghian
Associate Curator of Invertebrate Zoology
Santa Barbara Museum of Natural History

BEARPORT
PUBLISHING

NEW YORK, NEW YORK

Credits

Cover, © Ed Reschke/Photolibrary and © Pavel Lebedinsky; TOC, © Mashe/Shutterstock; 4–5, © Dwight Kuhn/Dwight Kuhn Photography; 6, © Bruce Davidson/Nature Picture Library; 7, © Paul Debois/Gap Photo/Visuals Unlimited, Inc.; 8T, © Dwight Kuhn/Dwight Kuhn Photography; 8B, © Dwight Kuhn/Dwight Kuhn Photography; 9, © Phil Degginger/Alamy; 10–11, © Ed Reschke/Photolibrary; 12–13, © David M. Dennis/Photolibrary; 14T, © Dwight Kuhn/Dwight Kuhn Photography; 14B, © Dwight Kuhn/Dwight Kuhn Photography; 15, © Dwight Kuhn/Dwight Kuhn Photography; 16, © Dwight Kuhn/Dwight Kuhn Photography; 17, © Tony Wharton/FLPA; 18–19, © Andrew Bailey/FLPA; 20–21, © Dwight Kuhn/Dwight Kuhn Photography; 22TL, © Robert Maier/Photolibrary; 22TR, © Peter Verhoog/Foto Natura/Minden Pictures/Getty Images; 22BL, © N A Callow/NHPA/Photoshot; 22BR, © Dr. John D. Cunningham/Visuals Unlimited, Inc.; 22spot, © Alle/Shutterstock; 23TL, © Jim Wehtje/Photodisc/Getty Images; 23TR, © Dwight Kuhn/Dwight Kuhn Photography; 23BL, © Dwight Kuhn/Dwight Kuhn Photography; 23BR, © Ed Reschke/Photolibrary; 24, © Dusty Cline/Shutterstock.

Publisher: Kenn Goin
Editorial Director: Adam Siegel
Creative Director: Spencer Brinker
Original Design: Dawn Beard Creative
Photo Researcher: Q2A Media: Farheen Aadil

Library of Congress Cataloging-in-Publication Data

Lunis, Natalie.
  Wiggly earthworms / by Natalie Lunis
      p. cm. — (No backbone! The world of invertebrates)
  Includes bibliographical references and index.
  ISBN-13: 978-1-59716-751-2 (library binding)
  ISBN-10: 1-59716-751-7 (library binding)
  1. Earthworms—Juvenile literature. I. Title.

QL391.A6L86 2009
592'.64—dc22
                              2008030827

For more information, write to Bearport Publishing Company, Inc., 101 Fifth Avenue, Suite 6R, New York, New York 10003. Printed in the United States of America.

10 9 8 7 6 5 4 3 2 1

Contents

Wet and Wiggly

Earthworms are covered with wet, slimy skin.

Their long, wiggly bodies have no legs and no bones.

Many people think they are gross.

Yet earthworms are one of the most important animals in the world.

Earthworms are
found all over the world.
They can live wherever
the soil is not frozen
or too dry.

5

Short and Long

There are about 4,900 kinds of earthworms.

The smallest is about one inch (2.5 cm) long.

The largest is 12 feet (3.6 m) long—about the same length as a big surfboard.

African giant earthworm

The best-known earthworm in the United States is about 6 inches (15 cm) long. Many people call this worm the *nightcrawler* because it stays underground during the day and comes out at night to eat.

nightcrawler

From End to End

An earthworm's body has a head end and a tail end.

In between are lots of little rings called segments.

Each segment has four pairs of tiny **bristles**.

The bristles help the worm grab hold of soil as it moves through the earth.

Earthworms have a thick band near their head end. The worms use mucus from this band to make cocoons that hold and protect their eggs until they hatch.

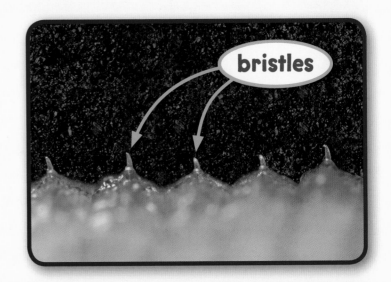

bristles

cocoon

segments

tail end

thick band

head end

9

On the Inside

Inside its body, an earthworm has a tiny brain, five pairs of hearts, and a long **intestine**.

The brain controls the worm's movements and helps it sense the world around it.

The hearts pump blood through the worm's body.

The intestine helps the worm turn food into fuel that its body can use.

Some kinds of earthworms have blood that is red, like human blood. The red blood gives these worms their reddish color.

hearts

brain

intestine

throat

mouth

Underground Living

Many kinds of earthworms live in underground tunnels.

To dig them, the worms push their long bodies through the soil.

Some dig tunnels that run just an inch or two (2.5 to 5 cm) below the ground.

Others, such as the nightcrawler, dig tunnels that go deep down into the ground.

A nightcrawler's tunnel can be six feet (2 m) deep.

By digging tunnels, earthworms help all kinds of plants to grow. How? They loosen the soil so that air and water can reach the roots.

13

Worm Food

Earthworms eat dead leaves and other pieces of rotting plants.

They also eat soil, seeds, and small twigs.

They have no teeth, so they suck the food into their mouths.

Inside their intestines, the parts that they cannot use are turned into waste called **castings**.

The castings pass out of an opening at the end of the worms' tail.

earthworm's mouth

leaf

Some of the food in a worm's intestine breaks down into tiny bits that can help plants grow. These bits make up part of a worm's castings. When a worm leaves its castings behind, the tiny bits go into the ground and make soil rich and healthy.

castings

Worms for Dinner

An earthworm's meaty body makes a good meal for many different animals.

Robins and other birds pull worms from their tunnels when they come out to eat.

Shrews, moles, and other furry animals that live in tunnels hunt them underground.

Toads, frogs, snakes, and skunks like to eat earthworms, too.

frog

mole

Moles catch earthworms and store them in their underground homes. Then, during the winter, when food is hard to find, the moles eat the worms.

Getting a Grip

An earthworm can't do much to defend itself from enemies that live underground.

It can try to save itself from a hungry bird, however.

Usually, the bird grabs the worm by the head end as the worm pokes out of the ground.

Using its body and its bristles, the worm grips the sides of its tunnel and holds on tight.

Sometimes it wins the struggle and is able to slip back into the earth.

A bird often bites off part of a worm while pulling on it. If the bitten-off part is from the head end, the worm usually dies. If the bitten-off part is from the tail end, it often grows back, and the worm survives.

Good for the Earth

Hundreds of earthworms can live below a small yard or garden.

That idea may seem gross, but in fact it's good news.

Earthworms are an important food for birds and other animals.

They help plants by bringing air, water, and rich matter into the soil.

Earthworms don't just live in the earth—they are good for the earth.

Some people raise worms and sell their castings to farmers, gardeners, and stores that sell gardening supplies. The people who buy the castings mix them into the soil to help plants grow.

A World of Invertebrates

An animal that has a skeleton with a **backbone** inside its body is a *vertebrate* (VUR-tuh-brit). Mammals, birds, fish, reptiles, and amphibians are all vertebrates.

An animal that does not have a skeleton with a backbone inside its body is an *invertebrate* (in-VUR-tuh-brit). More than 95 percent of all kinds of animals on Earth are invertebrates.

Some invertebrates, such as insects and spiders, have hard skeletons—called exoskeletons—on the outside of their bodies. Other invertebrates, such as worms and jellyfish, have soft, squishy bodies with no exoskeletons to protect them.

Here are four worms that are closely related to earthworms. Like all worms, they are invertebrates.

Leech

Clam Worm

Potworm

Marine Worm

Glossary

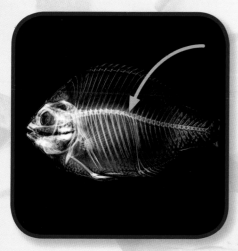

backbone
(BAK-bohn)
a group of
connected bones
that run along
the backs of some
animals, such as
dogs, cats, and fish;
also called a spine

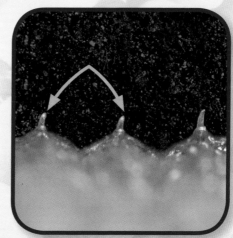

bristles
(BRISS-uhlz)
hair-like parts
on the outside of
an earthworm's
body

castings
(KAST-ingz)
waste that is
passed out of an
earthworm's body
after it eats

intestine
(in-TESS-tin)
the long,
tube-shaped part
on the inside of an
earthworm's body
where food is
turned into useful
fuel and waste

Index

Read More

Himmelman, John. *An Earthworm's Life*. New York: Children's Press (2000).

Llewellyn, Claire, and Barrie Watts. *Earthworms*. New York: Franklin Watts (2002).

Learn More Online

To learn more about earthworms, visit

www.bearportpublishing.com/NoBackbone–CreepyCrawlers

About the Author

Natalie Lunis has written many science and nature books for children. She lives in the Hudson River Valley, just north of New York City.

24